First World War
and Army of Occupation
War Diary
France, Belgium and Germany

60 DIVISION
Divisional Troops
Divisional Signal Company
21 June 1916 - 23 November 1916

WO95/3028/5

The Naval & Military Press Ltd
www.nmarchive.com
Published in association with The National Archives

Published by

The Naval & Military Press Ltd

Unit 10 Ridgewood Industrial Park,

Uckfield, East Sussex,

TN22 5QE England

Tel: +44 (0) 1825 749494

www.naval-military-press.com

www.nmarchive.com

This diary has been reprinted in facsimile from the original. Any imperfections are inevitably reproduced and the quality may fall short of modern type and cartographic standards.

© **Crown Copyright**
Images reproduced by permission of The National Archives, London, England, 2015.

Contents

Document type	Place/Title	Date From	Date To
Heading	WO95/3028/5		
Heading	War Diary 60th Division Signal Co. R.E.T From June 21st 1916 To June 30th 1916		
War Diary	On Board Transport Court Field	21/06/1916	21/06/1916
War Diary	Havre	22/06/1916	23/06/1916
War Diary	Flers	24/06/1916	24/06/1916
War Diary	Villers Chatel	27/06/1916	30/06/1916
Heading	War Diary Of 60th "Lon" Divl Signal Coy From 1st-31st July 1916 Vol II		
War Diary	Villers Chatel	01/07/1916	10/07/1916
War Diary	Hermaville	14/07/1916	31/07/1916
War Diary	Hermaville	02/08/1916	30/09/1916
Diagram etc	60th (London) Division		
War Diary	Hermaville	01/10/1916	26/10/1916
War Diary	Houvin Houvigneul	26/10/1916	28/10/1916
War Diary	Frohen-Le-Grand	29/10/1916	29/10/1916
War Diary	Bernaville	29/10/1916	31/10/1916
Diagram etc	Appendix A		
Heading	War Diary Of the 60th Div Signal Coy R.E (T) From 1st-30th November 1916 Volume VI		
War Diary	Bernaville	03/11/1916	03/11/1916
War Diary	Ailly-Le-Haute-Clocher	03/11/1916	23/11/1916

WO 95/3028/5

Secret.

War Diary

60th Division Signal Co., R.E. T.

From June 21st 1916 to June 30th 1916

Army Form C. 2118.

WAR DIARY
or
INTELLIGENCE SUMMARY

(Erase heading not required.)

Instructions regarding War Diaries and Intelligence Summaries are contained in F. S. Regs., Part II. and the Staff Manual respectively. Title Pages will be prepared in manuscript.

Place	Date	Hour	Summary of Events and Information	Remarks and references to Appendices
On board Transport Courtfield	21/6/16		Southampton H.Q. and No. 1 Section embarked at SOUTHAMPTON at 5 p.m.	
		10.30 p.m.	Submarine alarm – all hands ordered on deck till 12.30	
		a.m. (22nd)	when men allowed to return to quarters.	
HAVRE	22/6/16		Arrived at HAVRE 7 a.m. Disembarked and reached No. 2 Rest Camp 1.30 p.m.	
"	23/6/16		Entrained at HAVRE 11.30 a.m. Train left HAVRE station 2.10 p.m.	
FLERS	24/6/16	8.30 a.m.	Arrived at ST. POL. Detrained and marched to FLERS	
		12 noon	Arrived at FLERS. The men were put billets at CHATEAU HOME FARM. Established communication by telegraph and telephone with 3rd Army & 17th Corps.	
VILLERS CHATEL	27/6/16	7.30 a.m.	Left FLERS and marched to VILLERS CHATEL arriving 10.30 a.m. Established communication by telegraph and telephone with 7th Corps.	

Army Form C. 2118.

WAR DIARY
or
INTELLIGENCE SUMMARY

(*Erase heading not required.*)

Instructions regarding War Diaries and Intelligence Summaries are contained in F. S. Regs., Part II. and the Staff Manual respectively. Title Pages will be prepared in manuscript.

Place	Date	Hour	Summary of Events and Information	Remarks and references to Appendices
VILLERS CHATEL	27/6/16		2nd Infantry Brigade of 60th Div.	
"	30/6/16		2/Lt. Woodhouse & 25 other ranks proceeded to HERMAVILLE for temporary attachment to 51 Div. for instructional purposes, & to hold population in taking over communication of this divisional area.	
"				

60.

Vol II

Confidential.

War Diary of the 60th "a" Lon Divl.

Signal Coy from 1st — 31st July 1916.

Army Form C. 2118.

WAR DIARY
or
INTELLIGENCE SUMMARY
(Erase heading not required.)

Instructions regarding War Diaries and Intelligence Summaries are contained in F. S. Regs., Part II. and the Staff Manual respectively. Title Pages will be prepared in manuscript.

Place	Date	Hour	Summary of Events and Information	Remarks and references to Appendices
VILLERS CHATEL	1/7/16		O.C. Brigade Sections of Company ward & Bde. H.Q. of Brigades of 51st D.W. to make themselves acquainted with the communications of the Brigade area, prior to taking over.	Ea.
"	6/7/16		2nd Lt. W. WOODHOUSE & Woodhouse reported having duplicated the apparatus at S.W. H.Q. HERMAVILLE, & being thus ready to take over this office.	Ea.
"	10/7/16		2nd Lt. WOODHOUSE reports having duplicated apparatus at advanced S. H.Q. ETRUN. B.V. 2nd Lt. GRIST attached to 154th Bde. Signal Section, for the purpose of becoming acquainted with the communications of this Brigade area.	Ea.
HERMAVILLE	14/7/16	6.00 a.m.	The H.Q. & No. 1 Section of Company marched to HERMAVILLE. Took over Signal Office at HERMAVILLE from 51st S.W. Armoury. H.H.KING	Ea.
	17/7/16	10 a.m.	Capt. Anthony O.C. Bn. London Regts. (Work Office Dupt) reported to unit from S.6. D.W. Signal Coy.	Ea.

Army Form C. 2118.

WAR DIARY
or
INTELLIGENCE SUMMARY

(Erase heading not required.)

Instructions regarding War Diaries and Intelligence Summaries are contained in F. S. Regs., Part II. and the Staff Manual respectively. Title Pages will be prepared in manuscript.

Place	Date	Hour	Summary of Events and Information	Remarks and references to Appendices
HERMANVILLE	17/7/16	10.0 am	II Lt A GRIST returned to HQ Section.	a8
	20/7/16	11.0 am	R.E. Lyph Sct. 13 ORs arrived from G.H.Q	a8
	21/7/16	3.30 pm	Draft 8 OR's arrived from Base Signal Depot	a8
	23/7/16	11.0 am	Cm held on 14.32 Cpl MARRIOTT. S.	a8
	27/7/16	2.8 p	Award of Cm on 14.32 Cpl MARRIOTT S promulgated - Cpl MARRIOTT returned to ranks	a8
	29/7/16	Noon	MAUDSLEY motor lorry arrived from Divl Supply Col 2 ORs	a8
	30/7/16	11.00 am	Cm held at ETRUN on 20th Pk Wingrave 7.H. 17 Corps Cyclist Battn (attacked)	a8
	31/7/16	3.0 pm	4 ORs arrived from Base Signal Depot.	

Army Form C. 2118.

WAR DIARY or INTELLIGENCE SUMMARY

60TH Dv. SIGNAL Co R.E. T.

(Erase heading not required.)

Instructions regarding War Diaries and Intelligence Summaries are contained in F. S. Regs., Part II. and the Staff Manual respectively. Title Pages will be prepared in manuscript.

WL 3

Place	Date	Hour	Summary of Events and Information	Remarks and references to Appendices
HERMAVILLE	2/8/16	9.0 am	Award of CM on 20th to Wingrave F.H. 17 Corps Cyclist Battn promulgated. Sentence 2 months FP No 1 & 1 months extra forfeiture of pay - latter remitted by G.O.C. 1 O.R. left for AUBIGNY. 4 O.R. left for BERTHONVAL FARM to be attached to R.F.A. for constructional work	aj.
		5.55 am	Span of wires destroyed by shell fire at MAROEUIL Stn - Repaired	aj
		7.30 am	6 lines run from ETRUN	aj
	7/8/16	9.0 am	2 O.R.'s arrived from ABBEVILLE	aj
		11.0 am	1 O.R. do do	
		5 pm	No 12740 II Cpl WHITAKER R.C. admitted to hospital suffering from slight shrapnel wound.	aj
	8/8/16	6.0 pm	6 O.R.s arrived from G.H.Q. with two TRENCH WIRELESS SETS	aj
			6 O.R.'s evacuated to G.H.Q.	
	9/8/16	4.0 pm	H.M. The KING visited DIVISIONAL AREA	aj
		5.0 pm	1754 Sapper TAYLOR. J.C. wounded slightly leg evacuated Casualty Clg Stn	aj
	10/8/16	12.40 2.0 pm	II Cpl WHITAKER R.C. discharged to duty	aj

WAR DIARY
or
INTELLIGENCE SUMMARY

(Erase heading not required.)

Army Form C. 2118.

Place	Date	Hour	Summary of Events and Information	Remarks and references to Appendices
HERMAVILLE	16.8.16	2.0pm	1 C.R. arrived from BASE.	
	17.8.16	6	1 O.R. (MC) arrived from SIGNAL DEPOT.	
	20.8.16	do	3 O.R. arrived from SIGNAL DEPOT. Enemy	
	24.8.16	3.45pm	Two hostile shells fell in ARRAS - ST POL Road in communication with R. Army & CORPS. Reported to Corps Working Party.	
	27.8.16	8.0pm	6 O.R. as operators with trench Sets left per Corps Lorry for Alex RIETZ for duty.	

WAR DIARY or **INTELLIGENCE SUMMARY**
Army Form C. 2118.

60 D Signal Coy
H.Q 60th Signals R.E.T.
Vol 4

Place	Date	Hour	Summary of Events and Information	Remarks and references to Appendices
HERMAVILLE	1-9-16	1-15 pm to 1-39 pm	Enemy shelled ETRUN. One shell burst close to the Signal Office, breaking the windows and filling the office with smoke. 2/Lt B.W WOODHOUSE who was in the office, ordered all NCO's and men not actually on duty in the instrument room to take cover in the cellar, and himself remained in the switchroom with the man on duty, until the shelling ceased. Two shells pitched in the field near the MAROEUIL - ARRAS railway close to the new Signal dugout. One shell damaged a few wires but was speedily repaired and no delays occurred.	A.9.
	3-9-16	9 pm	No 751 Sgt J.C.Cox remustered as a Sapper. Suitable Telephonist Sappers for instruction for Battalion Signallers in Telephone working commenced	A.9 A.9
	7-9-16	2.0 p.m	Officer joined 2/Lt R.C. ANDERSEN.	A.9
	8-9-16	2.0 pm	The whole of the signal office (RC) was transferred from its old position in a house in ARCH STREET ETRUN to a new dugout in the east side of the railway cutting on MAROEUIL - ARRAS Railway.	A.9

WAR DIARY
or
INTELLIGENCE SUMMARY

(Erase heading not required.)

Army Form C. 2118.

Instructions regarding War Diaries and Intelligence Summaries are contained in F. S. Regs., Part II. and the Staff Manual respectively. Title Pages will be prepared in manuscript.

Place	Date	Hour	Summary of Events and Information	Remarks and references to Appendices
HERMAVILLE	5-07-16	2.0 a.m	The transfer was successfully accomplished on less than half an hour without any interruption of communication having been made previously for a temporary store and switchboard in the Chateau cellar. The new signal dugout proved to be completed £ 52 turn. All of which are lines in from distributor poles as shown in diagram Appendix "A"	A8
	26-7-16	10.00	Armoured Report centre ETRUN closed for telegraphic work. Circuits are now worked direct to Brigades from HERMAVILLE. This shortens operating time by eliminating transfers and giving a direct line to each Gen. Brigade H.Q. This was effected by superimposition of two telephone circuits from HERMAVILLE to ETRUN and the extension of the above circuit from HERMAVILLE to MT ST ELOY. Too much interruption by more current was found to occur on superimposed system of the line from HERMAVILLE to ECOIVRES but this was successfully overcome by the use of a Interphone.	A8

Army Form C. 2118.

WAR DIARY
or
INTELLIGENCE SUMMARY
(Erase heading not required.)

Place	Date	Hour	Summary of Events and Information	Remarks and references to Appendices
HERMAVILLE	27-9-16	6.0pm	Fullerphone classes finished. Each battalion in the division now has eight men trained in the use of this instrument	AS.
	30-9-16	7.0pm	3 O.R. joined from Signal Depot. 1 Officer joined the Coy. Capt H. H. KING to report his regt 1/18th Battn LONDON REGT.	AS
			GENERAL	
			During the month Buzzer Unit Exchanges have been introduced into HQ's of all Battns in the line, Brigade "support" and Brigade Signal Offices. Magneto Ringing Exchanges have been installed in all advanced Brigade HQrs, Signal Office in two of the Rear Bde HQrs and the Left Artillery Group leaving only two artillery groups and one Rear Brigade HQrs to be supplied.	AS

[signature] Major
R.E.T.
OC 60th Div Sig Coy.

2449 Wt. W14957/M90 750,000 1/16 J.B.C. & A. Forms/C.2118/12.

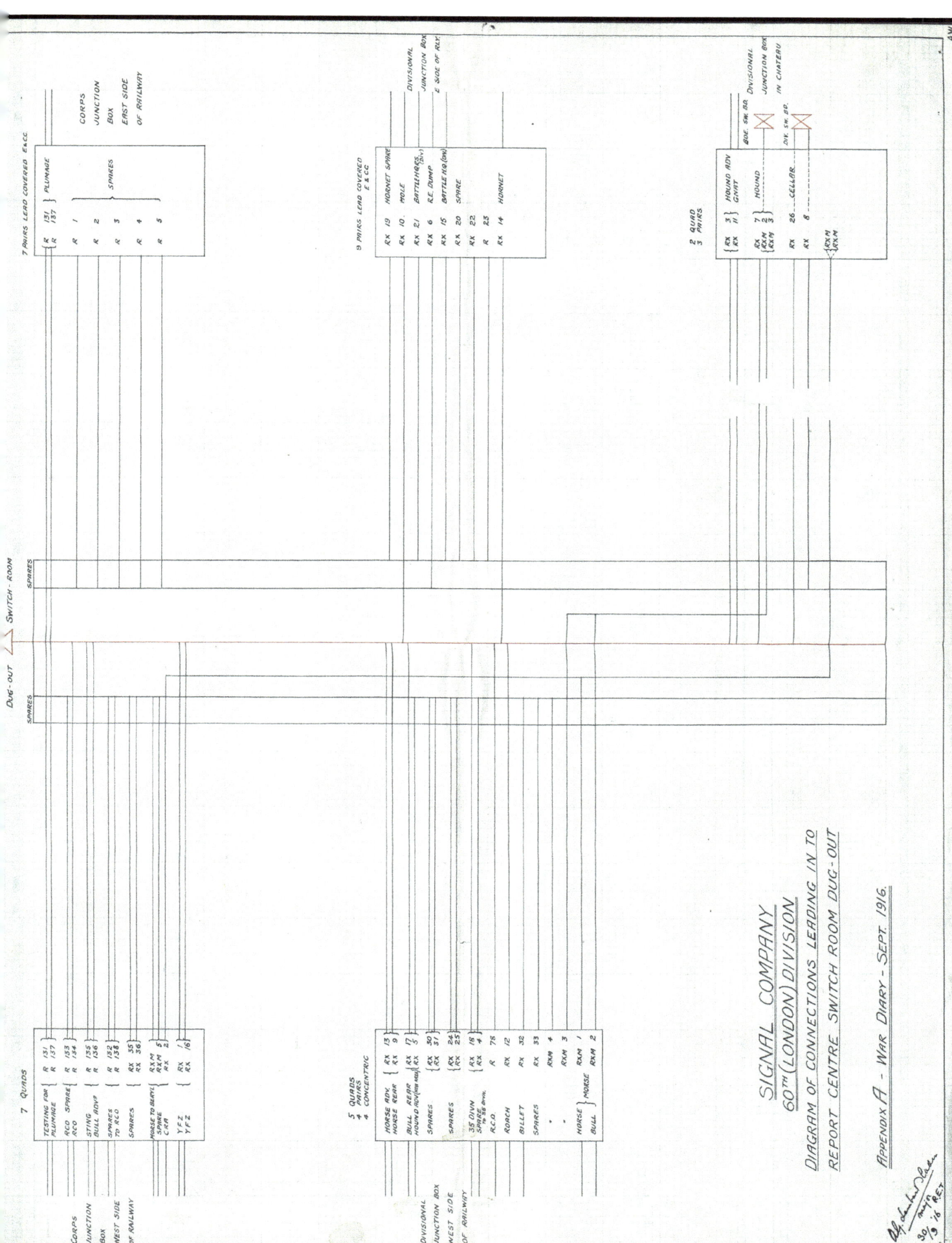

WAR DIARY
INTELLIGENCE SUMMARY
(Erase heading not required.)

Army Form C. 2118.

Signal Coy
HQ 60th Signal Co
Vol 5

Place	Date	Hour	Summary of Events and Information	Remarks and references to Appendices
HERMAVILLE	1.10.16	9.0 am	Buried line put in between 180th Bde and Royal Horse Artillery BERTONVAL FARM. SIC F4 d S.2	A.9
	5.10.16	4.0 pm	Substitution of air line for cable between Advanced Div. R.C. ETRUN and D.O.T.M. RÉ MAROEUIL	A.9
	7.10.16 & 8.10.16		Proceeding yesterday on 168th Cpl MERRIMAN J Grade3 1 OR arrived from BASE. Authority XVII Corps Cpl A.9. ref 5 7.10.16.	A.9
	12.10.16	11.30 am	1 O.R. mounted AUDRUICQ to TOMSKOW Station Rly opening Div	A.9
	13.10.16 from		Design and manufacture of a Portable TESTING SET by Lt. B.W. WOODHOUSE RE(T) - See appendix A.X	X A.9
	14.10.16		To determine hole to office route Multiple Earth substitution for air line	A.9
	16.10.16	7.0 am	Lt L.S. PALMER I/c No 4 Brigade Sec relieved by Lt R.C. ANDERSEN and joins HQ Section	A.9

Army Form C. 2118.

WAR DIARY
or
INTELLIGENCE SUMMARY

(Erase heading not required.)

Instructions regarding War Diaries and Intelligence
Summaries are contained in F. S. Regs., Part II.
and the Staff Manual respectively. Title Pages
will be prepared in manuscript.

Place	Date	Hour	Summary of Events and Information	Remarks and references to Appendices
HERMAVILLE	26-10-16	10.0 am	HQ and No 1 Section (Minus a full section detachment of 2 officers and 18 O.R.) proceeded to HOUVIN - HOUVIGNEUL by route march with HQ of 60th Div - Office closed.	
HOUVIN HOUVIGNEUL	26-10-16	10.0 am	opened office 10.0 am by advance party.	
do	do	11.45 pm	Coy arrived.	
do	28/10/16	6.0 pm	LT. J.N.R. PERKS joined from 1st Corps and proceeded to No 4 Brigade Section, vice 2 Lt ANDERSEN - who rejoined HQ Section.	
			LT PALMER left for 1st Corps.	
do	28/10/16	10.0 am	Office closed at 10.0 am - Coy proceeded by route march	
FROHEN- LE-GRAND	28/10/16	10.0 am	Office opened 10.0 am. Coy arrived 1.0 pm	
do	29-10-16	10.0 am	Office closed. Coy proceeded by route march	
BÉANAVILLE	do	10.0 am	Office opened 10.0 am - Coy arrived 12.15 pm.	
do	30/10/16	8.0 am	3 O.R. arrived	
do	31/10/16	9.30 am	2 Lt R. ANDERSEN left for HERMAVILLE to relieve Lt ANDREWES in charge of 1 Corps Arty Communications.	
do	do	9.15 pm	LT ANDREWES joined HQ Section	

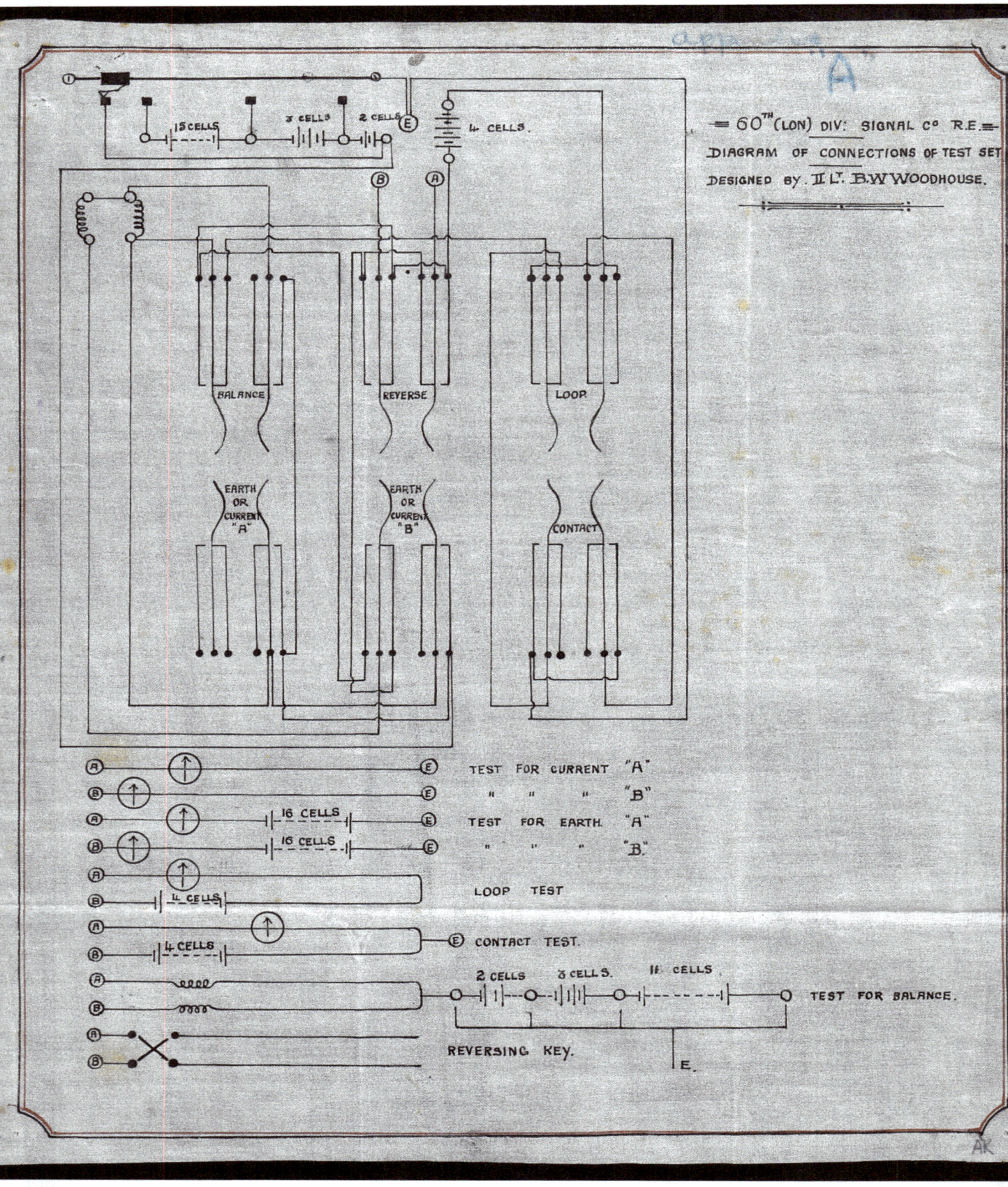

Vol 6

Confidential

War Diary of the
60th Div Signal Coy RE(T)
from 1st – 30th November 1916.

Volume VI

Army Form C. 2118.

WAR DIARY
or
INTELLIGENCE SUMMARY 60th Div Signal Coy RE(T)

(Erase heading not required.)

Instructions regarding War Diaries and Intelligence Summaries are contained in F. S. Regs., Part II. and the Staff Manual respectively. Title Pages will be prepared in manuscript.

Place	Date	Hour	Summary of Events and Information	Remarks and references to Appendices
BERNAVILLE	3-11-16	9.30 am	Office closes 9.30 am. Coy proceeded by route march to AILLY-LE-HAUTE-CLOCHER.	A8
AILLY-LE-HAUTE-CLOCHER	3-11-16	9.30	Office opened by Advance Party. Coy arrived 12.50 pm	A8
do	do	9.30	Orders received for reorganization of Coy on War Establishment Part 12 SALONIKA 4.	A8
do	15-11-16		25 O.R. arrived from SIGNAL DEPÔT to complete establishment	Born
	19-11-16		Headquarters, N°1 Officer, 1 Sg O.R, 33 animals & vehicles entrained LONPRÉ for MARSEILLES	Born
			N°1 Section, 6 Officers, 71 OR, 45 animals & vehicles entrained at LONPRÉ for MARSEILLES	Born
	20-11-16		Headquarters arrive MARSEILLES & proceed to VALENTINO CAMP	Born
	22-11-16			Born
	23-11-16		N° 1 Section arrive MARSEILLES 7 am. Moved Camp FOURNIER	Born

[signature]
Major
O/C 60th Signal Coy RE(T)

2449 Wt. W14957/Mg0 750,000 1/16 J.B.C. & A. Forms/C.2118/12.